Angels Don't Die

ANGELS
DON'T DIE

MY FATHER'S
GIFT OF FAITH

PATTI DAVIS

HarperCollins*Publishers*

FIRST EDITION

Designed by Nancy Singer

Library of Congress Cataloging-in-Publication Data

Davis, Patti
 Angels don't die / Patti Davis.—1st ed.
  p. cm.
 ISBN 0-06-017324-6
 1. Davis, Patti. 2. Reagan, Ronald. 3. Children of presidents—United States—Biography. 4. Authors, American—20th century—Biography. I. Title.
E878.D38A3 1995
973'.099—dc20   95-10358
[B]

---

95 96 97 98 99 ❖/HC 10 9 8 7 6 5 4 3 2 1

This book is dedicated to my father, who told me as a child that there was a Father in Heaven, and I didn't have to stand on my toes to touch Him. And to my mother—we have taken a tangled path to come finally into a clearing where Love had been waiting for us all along.

Acknowledgments

Thank you to Flip Brophy for believing in this book from the beginning; to Diane Reverand for taking it under her wing; to Jack McKeown for saying yes. Thank you also to Cindy Rakowitz for reading an early draft and finding the title in the text. Special thanks to my parents for their contributions.

I've always believed that we were, each of us, put here for a reason; that there is a plan, somehow a divine plan for all of us. In an effort to embrace that plan, we are blessed with the special gift of prayer, the happiness and solace to be gained by talking to the Lord. It is our hopes and our aspirations, our sorrows and fears, our deep remorse and renewed resolve, our thanks and joyful praise, and most especially our love, all turned toward a loving God. Many of us have been taught to pray by people we love. In my case, it was my mother. I learned quite literally at her knee. My mother gave me a great deal, but nothing she gave me was more important than that. She was my inspiration and provided me with a very real and deep faith.

Ronald Reagan

When you're in the public eye, people think they know you—who you are, what you're made of, what you're like. In an attempt to define me over the years many have examined me from this angle or that, but the truth is they've never really known the whole me. They've never caught a glimpse of the real Nancy because I keep a certain part of myself safely hidden from view. It's the essence of my faith that's sheltered, never spoken but fiercely guarded. I've drawn from that source countless times in the course of my life, during periods of great personal crisis and darkness. And while I was being tested, my faith revealed itself time and time again, giving me strength. Yes, it's true that I often prefer silence; but with faith as my crutch I've found peace, one of the few things I have left which is strictly my own.

Nancy Reagan

Prologue

I asked my father once—I think I must have been eight or nine—if it were true that every time a star falls it means an angel has died. Someone had told me that, and I was quite upset about it. I imagined Heaven being emptied out. I pictured God walking down endless, empty hallways calling out for angels who were no longer there. I remember brooding about this for days before finally asking my father.

"Angels don't die," he told me, to my great relief.

"So they'll always be there, to keep God company?" I asked. "So He'll never get lonely?"

"Yes," he assured me. "They'll always be there to keep God company. They can't die."

He then explained to me the scientific reality of what had happened, light-years before, that gives us the image of a falling star. I didn't care about the astronomy lesson, and I don't think I really paid attention to it. All I needed to know was that angels couldn't die.

Angels, in their ethereal wisdom, can

probably take whatever form they want. They can take the form of a story that floats into your life on white wings at exactly the moment when things look terrifyingly dark. It's been that way with some of my father's stories—they were there in my memory, but they fluttered into my life just when I needed them.

Storytelling has ancient roots. It's primal; stories live in your bones and your blood. They teach lessons, point the way, light candles in the blackest nights. They live on the wind and follow the seasons. Any good storyteller knows that he is a teacher. What my father taught me had to do with God and a world beyond this one. I etched some of those stories on the cave walls of my mind and then rolled a rock in front of the opening to that cave. Recently, I rolled the rock away, and those stories are still there, in faint lines and in bold colors. Stories, like angels, don't die.

Years ago, *60 Minutes* did a piece on my father in which they took some of the stories he had told in various speeches as if they had happened, and traced each one to an old movie or novel. I thought it was one of the meanest pieces I'd ever seen.

There was one story I had heard often before, during my childhood. It was about a young soldier and a chaplain in World War II, in a plane that had been hit and was going down in flames. Everyone else had been killed, and there was only one chute. The soldier was wounded and insisted that the chaplain, who was not, take the chute and save his life. The chaplain refused, telling the boy that they would go down together. *60 Minutes* ferreted around in old movie archives and came up with a clip that proved their point: that this story was not real life, it was movie life, and—come on, America—what does that say about Ronald Reagan?

But *60 Minutes* missed the point. The value of that story to my father was that it contains a message that is very real. People can lead with their hearts, they can act from Love, they can act in a God-inspired way. That ability is in all of us, whether we're going through the routine of our daily lives or staring death in the face. We might feel it as only a whisper, but it's there. The story is real in the most important way—in the lesson it imparts about who we really are as human beings, or at least who we can be. I loved that story—it is a good war story and a good message story, and it tells a truth that my father has never doubted. It says, "God created us in His image. That means we're supposed to be like Him. And God would never parachute away from a dying man."

I used to watch my father as he watched the sky, and I would wonder where he was. His eyes were as blue and distant as the sky he was looking at. Much of my childhood was spent trying to sail across that distance. As usually happens, the answer was right there all the time—he was talking to God. He was praying. I think I get the same look in my own eyes now. Sometimes, in the midst of it, I thank my father for turning my attention upward, where I might get a glimpse of God catching one of my prayers like a firefly on its way to Heaven. That's what he told me prayers look like—fireflies that God reaches out to catch. I don't know whether that image came from a movie or a book, nor do I care. It's a good story, and on some nights, I'm sure that's what I see.

Angels Don't Die

I

My father taught me to talk to God, and taught me that prayer is exactly that—a conversation with God. This wasn't formal instruction; he simply described his own spiritual relationship in such a way that I was left with the impression that God was his friend, and they had deep, unstructured dialogues. When I was a child, it made perfect sense; now that I am an adult, it makes even more. I find myself praying in the same way, and describing the experience in similar terms to those my father used—"The answer I got was . . ." You ask, and God answers. My father made it seem simple, and I accepted that it was. I've always known that my way of praying came from my father's influence, but it took me years to say it, and years to thank him for this gift. Which is both the beginning and the end of this story.

"You taught me that prayer means talking with God," I told him on a February night two days before his eighty-third birthday. "I've never thanked you for the gift of faith you gave me."

His eyes filled up. "I didn't know. And I always wondered about your faith. Thank you for telling me."

I saw that, just as he had given me an invaluable gift, I in turn had given him something precious by acknowledging it and by giving him a sense of who I am. I think this is often the way things unfold with our parents. We go years assuming they're not honoring or respecting who we are, but we haven't let them know who we are. They don't know any more than what we've shown them.

When I was about nineteen or twenty, my father and I were in the midst of a conversation about some tragedy that had just occurred—an airline crash, I think. My father said, "It's always difficult to think that God has a reason for such things, but that's what faith is about. Of course, people like you who are atheists don't see it that way."

"Why are you assuming I'm an atheist?" I asked. "Because I've probed and asked questions? Or because I don't go to church?" I was young and arrogant about my right to question whatever I wanted. I didn't feel I should have to explain or label myself.

"Well, I just assumed," my father answered in a soft voice—waiting, I know now, for an answer from me that he didn't get.

I could have told him that I had long conversations with God before falling asleep at night, and during the day as well, especially if the sky was doing something spectacular; that I had been having these conversations for years, for as long as I could remember. I could have told him that whenever I witnessed an exquisite sunset, or a dramatic arrangement of clouds, I thanked God for His artistry. I could have told him, but I didn't. And that's really what he was asking.

Years later, I woke up abruptly from a nightmare; I must have started crying during the dream, because my face was streaked with tears. The man I was living with woke up and tried to comfort me. He asked what I had dreamt that had upset me so. "I dreamed that my father said he didn't think I believed in God," I answered, still sobbing.

If dreams can sometimes hold up a dark mirror to the soul, they can just as often illuminate and instruct. The Talmud says, "A dream which is not understood is like a letter which is not opened." I was being given a message in that dream; I held it, still sealed, up to the light, but it would take almost twenty years for me to open it, read the message, and act upon it. When I sat with my father, just before his eighty-third birthday, I finally answered his question about my faith. I finally acknowledged him and thanked him for the gift of faith he had given me.

It was one of those pivotal moments. A story that had just been a shadow in my mind insisted on being written.

I have said that, as a writer, I had finished drawing on my family experiences for material. But as every writer knows, some chapters wait in the wings. They don't scream at you or make demands, they just wait for you to find them. I had been keeping a journal of the spiritual lessons and insights that had been flickering on in my life, like candles lighting up a dark room. I began to notice that I could trace all of these lessons back to things my father had taught me. I didn't know exactly how this journal would grow or what form it would eventually take. That night, after I spoke with my father, I knew.

The world knows much about Ronald Reagan; it should also be known that he passed along to his daughter a deep, resilient faith that God's love never wavers, and that no matter how harsh life seems, or how cruel the world is, that love is constant, unconditional, and eternal. The world should know that Ronald Reagan was a father who patiently answered his child's questions about God, and angels, and miracles. That child grew into an adult who has never doubted the possibility of miracles and the presence of God, and who hears her father's answers even when the dark times seem overwhelming.

The reason this story is focused primarily on my father is fairly basic: He was the one who talked openly and freely about spiritual matters. I know my mother has her beliefs and her own way of communicating with God, but it's a part of herself that she holds close, which is her right.

In matters concerning God, my mother preferred the shady side of the street, where her feelings wouldn't be exposed to bright light, where she could keep them private. As a child, with an endless stream of questions about nonearthly things, I crossed to the sunnier side, where my father spun stories about Heaven and angels, and drew maps in the dirt with signs saying, "This way to God."

Now I see that my mother's spiritual life was not as much in shadow as I thought. She lit a candle in the window, so that no matter how far-flung my father's prayers were, how far beyond the clouds they soared, they had a place to come home to—a point of arrival and departure, a warm hearth and a safe bed . . . and a reminder that prayers can be answered on earth, too, not just in the blue reaches of his imagination. She kept people away from him on airplanes, at takeoffs and landings, because she knew at those moments he wasn't just looking out the window—he was praying. She was the sentry at the gate—don't intrude, this is a holy moment (although she probably didn't say it like that). And she carved a moat around the purest acreage of his character. Like a warning sign outside a nature preserve—don't pollute, don't litter. There is an old saying:

"Ignorance is not knowing anything and being attracted to the good. Innocence is knowing everything and still being attracted to the good." My father's nature has never lost its innocence, not because he's a stranger to betrayal or meanness but because he has chosen to look for the good. My mother patrolled the grounds, looking for dark intruders, banishing them if they encroached on his light.

Miracles can always be ushered in; they only require faith and a willingness to be open to them, to allow room in one's life for the miraculous to occur. The writing of this book has been like a deep breath that expanded the boundaries of my life and my heart, and I have been humbled and, at moments, driven to my knees in gratitude for the presence of God's hand, holding miracles in His palm. One of the most profound has been the way this story—and my life—has molded itself around a relationship with my mother that I never thought I would have. We have never been mild with each other—in our anger as well as in our love we have been intense, bonded, joined at the corners of our souls. Finally, we stepped into a circle of light where only Love was allowed to enter. It seems so perfect to me now that she has taken her place in this story, guided it in some ways; I can't remember seeing it any other way.

She has told me things about the day my father was shot, and the aftermath—invaluable stories that supported my ideas about what he had gone through. She revealed other things to me as well—fragments dropped into conversations. I have had to be quick with my memory and my pen.

She told me about her love for the ocean. No wonder, I thought—the summers when our family rented a beach house were purifying, sacred, as holy as baptisms to me. I remember one summer evening, looking out the window at my parents sitting on the sand, close together, gazing out to sea, their faces tilted toward the sunset spilling across the horizon. I watched them with the same reverence I felt for the sunset. I knew I was looking at something precious. I prayed at the moment that I would be blessed with as strong a love in my life—someone who would turn me toward sunsets and oceans and glorious horizons. And who could sit quietly with me, taking it all in.

Most important, my mother read this book in manuscript form, wept at what she read, and told me, "I hope it's published." Right then, I knew it would be. Blessings are important, and this book would not have been complete without hers.

One of the things my mother reminded me of was that my father has always preferred living on a hill, where he has a feeling of openness around him. Closer to the sky, I thought when she told me. I grew up in a house that sat high above Los Angeles, and behind us were other hills, even higher.

When I was a child, my father used to take me up to one of those hills to fly kites. One day I stood on my tiptoes and asked how tall I'd have to be to touch God.

He replied, "You don't need to be tall. God is all around—everywhere, all the time. He just waits for us to turn to Him. You don't even need to reach up. You just need to talk to Him, and listen to His answers."

"But what if I want to hold His hand?" I asked, my arm still stretched up to the blue sky that Los Angeles used to have.

"You still don't need to reach up to do

that," my father said. "But if you want to, you can."

I walked down the hill that day with my arm reaching up to the heavens. It wasn't that I doubted my father, I just wanted to improve the odds.

When I decided to write this book, I went through the questioning stage that is probably typical. Acting on the assumption that it's perfectly normal to conduct a survey of various friends before embarking on a project, I asked a few of mine.

One friend suggested that I structure the book in a chronological way—childhood up to now, linear, a straight shot through the years. But there are different types of chronology. Some of the spiritual insights I absorbed from my father I got right at the moment—at age nine, or ten, or fourteen. Others simmered for a while, or lay dormant, waiting for me to catch up, be ready for them before they dusted themselves off and walked into the sunlight.

There is no linear progression to this kind of story. It unfolds as a hilly landscape that doesn't reveal everything about itself at first glance.

For a brief time, when my father was governor of California, he kept his horses at a ranch just outside Sacramento. One day we rode together on the flat, open land where my vision stretched like elastic because there seemed to be no markers, no end, just one long wave of weeds in the afternoon wind. He said, "I'm not crazy about riding on flat land like this. You can always see what's ahead. There are never any surprises."

The landscape of my relationship with my father has been one of mountains, of things not seen until I rounded a bend, braved a new path, peered over the edge of some precipice. Then something about him—something that came from him—would be waiting for me. At first the discovery would seem like a surprise, but on deeper reflection, there was no surprise. His voice has always been there, floating through my life; I wasn't always listening.

I think as daughters we mythologize our fathers. We give them a larger voice, a larger presence than they feel comfortable with, and then we expect them to live up to that. We don't realize that we have placed upon them a terrible burden. If there is anything different about having a father who is enormously famous, who has climbed onto one of the highest pedestals the world has to offer, it's that the myth becomes larger, sturdier, harder to see through. The public voice booms from television and radio, is immortalized in print, and inevitably in history. But to really know someone, you have to listen to him in the smaller moments, and with a more discerning ear. Like listening to an orchestra but picking out the notes of one violin.

Since I was fathered by a public man who was destined to become even more public, I grew up with his voice booming around me, from all facets of the media. I let it drown out his quieter voice, the song beneath the myth.

I have learned now that the mythology doesn't work after a while. We end up running after the wind, chasing phantoms we created ourselves, which have little to do with who our fathers really are.

I don't necessarily subscribe to the theory that women look for their fathers in other men. I think the truth is we decide at some point who our fathers are—we construct a paint-by-numbers picture according to our own needs—and we expect them to fill in the colors. When the colors aren't what we had in mind, we become reactive—soldiers looking for a war. Other men become our weapons.

Louise Erdrich, in the poem entitled "Mary Magdalene," wrote:

> It is the old way that girls
> get even with their fathers—
> by wrecking their bodies on other men.

And the damage gets costly, I thought when I read those lines, particularly because all we're getting even with are our own illusions.

I try to look carefully now at the wreckage of romances that I've left in my wake; I try to search through the rubble for clues. I figure if I look at them with a clear eye, they'll turn into talismans—they'll protect me from damage in the future. And what I'm realizing is that the most disastrous romantic choices had little to do with who my father is; they had to do with my ignorance of who he is, and of the gifts I was meant to receive from him. It was as if I had been standing in front of a mountain, looking at rock formations, blind to the deep veins of gold running through them.

When I finally allowed myself to embrace the gifts that were there for me all along, my life changed, my ideas about men changed . . . because my ideas about myself changed. Before, I felt like open, unprotected territory, where hunters and poachers could blaze in with weapons or prowl the nights looking for their prey. Now, I feel like there's a white line circling my outermost boundaries; it's not mined, it doesn't glow in the dark, it's faint as thread, but certain people just aren't able to cross it. Opening myself to who my father is ultimately meant opening myself to who I am, and to the things that will enrich my life.

So, it's a journey, I suppose—a process of growing past the myths, the larger-than-life illusions, the stuff of fairy tales to a smaller, quieter realization that there has been a softer voice all along. It's been hanging on the wind like an echo. If we want to know our fathers, we have to stand still, quiet the drums, and listen. When I finally stopped and listened, I heard deeper harmonies and sweeter notes.

The truth of him is revealed in his stories, in the way he talks about God, and in small moments that have been preserved in my memory like fossils in rock.

There is a story that my father told me when I was a child, but I remember asking him to repeat it again and again. It's laced into the years. And it may explain more about Ronald Reagan than anything else.

It happened when he was a young actor, working on a film in England. He was asleep in his hotel room, he said, when he woke up—abruptly, as if something had jolted him out of sleep. He sat up in bed and had the unmistakable feeling that someone was behind him. But when he tried to turn around, he couldn't. Physically, he was unable to move, as though hands were on his shoulders, holding him in place.

"But suddenly, I didn't want to turn around anymore," he said. "I knew that whomever or whatever was behind me was there to protect me. I had the most amazing feeling of peace. I knew I was completely safe, and that I was loved."

"Was it God?" I used to ask him.

He would just smile.

There were nights, when I was a child, when I prayed for something like that to happen to me. I wanted those hands on my shoulders, I wanted that feeling of bliss and serenity. I wanted to know, in a tangible way, that God and His angels were behind me, even at night in my bedroom, where, as every child knows, monsters can set up residence and conduct a reign of terror that parents never seem to believe.

I still wish that sometimes. Because now that I am an adult, the monsters are worse. They're more clever, and they make the nights seem even darker. I've prayed for a miracle like the one that visited my father so many years ago.

But one night I realized something. There *were* hands on my shoulders; there always have been. The very fact that I was praying was evidence of that. The hands belonged, in a way, to my father, because he guided me to God at such a young age I never doubted that I have a Father in Heaven as well, and that He feels only love for me and the rest of His children.

*　　　*　　　*

When I discussed this book with another friend, she pointed out that some people might assume I was writing a eulogy of sorts. "Not to dissuade you," she added quickly, "but you should be prepared for it."

So I started thinking about eulogies, and about the friends I know who are also watching their parents grow older. It occurred to me that we are all, in our own fashions, writing eulogies for our parents, even in the small gestures, the moments of affection we didn't take time for before. We try to clean things up, put things in perspective, and hope to end up with something more poetic, more lyrical, which is, after all, what eulogies are supposed to be.

Perhaps our parents, whether they share this with us or not, are doing the same thing. They're thinking about time, too—about what's gone by and what remains. They smooth things out, tell more inspiring stories and abandon the more troubling ones. That's what I see my father doing.

He mentions "days dwindling down," and he mentions his age, and I see a wistfulness, a moment of longing that flutters across his face or hums beneath his words. But then—usu-ally—it's gone. More often, he treats aging with humor, joking about the historic figures he knew—"You know, when I had lunch with Thomas Jefferson . . ."

My father has always understood the value of humor. It's a tonic, and at times a life raft. Humor dulls the edges, makes life smoother, lets it go down easier. Which is sort of how my father looks much of the time—as if he's just swallowed something delicious, that went down smoothly and easily. He's always had it—America will probably never forget the "honey, I forgot to duck" line when he was shot—but his humor seems even sweeter to me now, smoother than it's ever been. A life milk shake.

When I heard that my father released a statement disputing Oliver North's account of what went on during Iran-Contra, and dis-tanced himself from North's campaign for senator, I thought, "This is Ronald Reagan the man—not the former president—cleaning up some of the messiness of the past, putting things in order, looking at the life he's lived in the same way some of us look at our closets—

this can go, this doesn't fit me anymore." He wasn't willing just to let North's comments slide, because once you really feel the pull of your own mortality, you think beyond it to what will be remembered, what will be spoken about and repeated.

It may be that eulogies start a while before death. At least they do if we're lucky enough to look down the road and see it getting shorter—if life doesn't end in one unexpected, fiery moment, a page-one *New York Times* moment of gunfire, or explosives in a parking structure. If life plays out as it's supposed to, eulogies are composed over years, by the people who are aging and by those who are watching them.

I see now that I've been collecting moments and memories for years now—stringing them together like the add-a-pearl necklace I had when I was a little girl. Some of the moments seem small, but they were very much like pearls. They shone with the luster of who my father was beneath the public person. A pearl has colors—it's not just white—but you have to hold it up to the light in just the right way to see them. It's the same with some of my memories, some of those seemingly small moments. The light is deeper now, richer, because I'm older and see from a different perspective, and now I notice more colors.

There was a moment, many years ago—perhaps I was ten, I'm not really sure—when my father whispered to me, early on Valentine's Day morning, that he'd forgotten to buy my mother a card. He looked like a boy arriving to pick up his date for the prom but without a corsage because he'd forgotten it. He was embarrassed, and felt ashamed. I remember offering to go into my room and make him one—I was very into drawing and painting at the time. "No, no, that's okay," he said, shaking his head slowly. "I'll figure something out."

I don't know what he figured out, or how he handled it, because the beauty of that moment was what it revealed about him—that even as a married adult, he could feel like a shy boy who wants to impress his date. I glimpsed the man who had fallen in love, who had called up for a date and arrived at the door with all the nervousness that goes along with first dates. Obviously, this dating phase of my parents' lives was before my time, but I saw a hint of it that morning. I think the reason this memory stands out for me is that it was the first time I considered the fact that my father had been that nervous young man on a date. A lot of life had been lived before he became my father. Maybe what made the moment so memorable was the realization that there were aspects to his character which had nothing to do with the fact that he was my father.

Another such moment happened many years later, when he was running for president. During a television interview he was asked about his divorce from Jane Wyman and the aftermath, the time before he married my mother. "It wasn't so much that I missed having someone to love me," he said, "as I missed having someone to give my love to."

I was struck by how pure that sentiment was. Rather than looking at what he was or was not getting for himself, he was focused on the beauty of giving love, which he wasn't able to do in that in-between-marriages time. He was focused on the most divine aspect of love—that of giving. I saw on his face the vulnerability, the loneliness he must have experienced during that time. No wonder God rewarded him with the gift of a deep, lasting love—he was a magnet for it.

In my autobiography, *The Way I See It,* I wrote about my reaction to a comment my father made on the day of my grandfather's funeral. My mother and I had put my grandmother to bed, and I had come out of the bedroom crying. My father looked at my tears and asked, "Why are you crying?" I felt that he didn't want to deal with the grief, that he was finding a way to escape it, deny it for the moment. But I see it differently now. I think he may have been revealing his own attitude about death through that question—that death is not really something to be sad about. It's a passage, a homecoming. God decides it's time to take one of His children home. Now, I feel that my father did understand from a worldly perspective why I was crying, but at that moment his perspective was spiritual. From that angle, there was nothing to cry about.

I string together moments like these, paying close attention to their colors, holding them up to the light in just the right way, because reflected in each one is the face of God.

"God always listens, and He's always watching," my father has told me often through the years, letting me know that this is one of the cornerstones of his life. The private man, beneath the public one, has always felt hands on his shoulders, keeping him safe, and he has never doubted that they belong to God.

2

My mother has told me that Cardinal Cooke assured my father, after he was shot in March of 1981, that he "had an angel sitting on his shoulder." It makes perfect sense to me now, knowing how close he came to death, how the surgeons almost couldn't find the bullet, how he almost slipped into shock. I didn't know this on the morning following the shooting, as I walked toward his hospital room with so many emotions churning in me it was hard to decipher all of them. The one that screamed at me was fear. I knew he had lost a lot of blood, and my mother had told me he almost died. I wish I'd known about the angel on his shoulder, I might have felt better. As it was, I was frightened to see my father weak or injured.

He had always appeared invincible to me—part of the mythology I had clung to, I suppose. When I went horseback riding with him, he could handle any situation that came up. He built jumps from fallen trees, hacked trails through thick brush. I was afraid to see him look frail. What I didn't know, as I approached his room, was that I was about to be given the clearest lesson in forgiveness I had ever witnessed.

He actually didn't look frail; he looked almost ethereal. There was a light in his eyes that made me think, then and still, that he saw something—visited with God, listened to the counsel of an angel—something. My mother has since told me that he woke up at one point after the doctors had operated on him, unable to talk because there was a tube down his throat. He saw figures in white standing around him and scrawled on a piece of paper, "I'm alive, aren't I?" My mother still has the note.

This story has become one that gathers more truth as it is shared with more listeners. When my mother first told it to me, we discussed how logical it is to assume that the figures in white, standing around my father, were the doctors and nurses who were tending to him. But maybe not, we said; maybe he did see angels. We left it with a question mark. Then I repeated it to a friend—a nurse—who pointed out to me that no one in a recovery room or in intensive care is in white; they're all in green scrubs. I phoned my mother and told her, and her reaction was "I didn't even think of that, there was so much that day—but you're right." I give endless prayers of thanks to whatever angels circled my father, because a Devastator bullet, which miraculously had not exploded, was finally found a quarter inch from his heart. Without divine intervention, I don't know if he would have survived.

Since I did not know this story at the time, what struck me most the following day was something my father said. He said he knew his physical healing was directly dependent on his ability to forgive John Hinckley. I remember telling him, "You're the best Christian around." My response was a pale shadow of my true feelings, which were so enormous I couldn't fit them into the boundaries of language.

By showing me that forgiveness is the key to everything, including physical health and healing, he gave me an example of Christ-like thinking. Forgiving is the antidote for anger, fear, and every form of hatred. I think of it as a force so huge, so powerful, that it can only lead to miracles. It is hard work, some of the hardest I've ever done, but my father made it sound effortless. His statement about forgiving Hinckley was clear and simple—a certainty he thought he'd share with the rest of us.

It saddens me that much of what passes as Christianity these days is not about Christlike thinking and is leagues away from forgiveness.

A couple of years ago, a friend told me that she had been invited to a charity Christmas event to be held at one of the more elegant Los Angeles hotels. The catch was, it was designated "Christians Only." I said to her, "Well, that kind of says it all, doesn't it?" It was one of the most uncharitable sentiments I'd ever heard; I cannot picture Jesus at the doors of a temple saying, "Sorry, I'd love to take your money, but you're a Moslem, so you'll have to leave."

During my father's administration, some prominent figures from the Religious Right rallied around him, aligned themselves with him, and probably left some with the impression that they all belonged to the same club, held to the same dogma, and listened to Jerry

Falwell on Sunday mornings. My father's statement about forgiving the man who shot him demonstrates that he has embraced the essence of Christ's teachings. He was revealing the core of his spirituality. I haven't heard anything remotely resembling that from the Religious Right.

I think about his words often, whenever some small slight or huge betrayal tempts me to be unforgiving. I know that if my father could forgive under those circumstances, I can do no less. If I go backwards, follow threads across the fabric of my memory, I can see that my father showed me how this is not just a principle to be used in dramatic, life-and-death circumstances. Seemingly inconsequential situations can often be invitations for noble emotions. My father used to say that heroes are frequently people who in everyday life take a moment to help someone else. Mother Teresa has been quoted as saying, "There are no great deeds. There are only small deeds done with great love." And so it is with forgiveness, I think. The lesson takes shape in the everyday moments, in life's abrupt snags.

We live in a world that thrives on drama. We tell ourselves that the small, mundane moments don't matter. I never saw my father ignore those small moments, or act as if they didn't count.

When I was a child, we had a routine of going out to the ranch on Saturdays. The property was in Agoura, inland from Malibu—three hundred and fifty acres of fields and pastures, ponds and oak groves—the paradise of my childhood. Occasionally, we would spend the night in the small ranch house with creaky floors—a house I still dream about. There was another routine—we would always stop for ice cream at a stand along the Coast Highway. I remember on one Saturday afternoon, the person selling ice cream was very rude to us for no apparent reason. When we got back to the car, my father said, "You know, you can never know what's going on in another person's life. That woman might have just gotten terrible news, or lost a loved one. Or maybe she's ill. Maybe that's why she was acting like that. You just never know."

The other day I went to the grocery store, which is one of my least favorite things to do—right up there with paying taxes or going to the dentist. To make matters worse, I was having a bad day altogether, and I just wanted to get my groceries and leave. But the girl at the check-out stand wanted to chat. She was remarking on what I'd bought, what she assumed I would be cooking. She was telling me about recipes she'd discovered, or invented, or liked. At any rate, she was trying to engage me in a conversation I didn't want to have and was not in the mood for, particularly since I didn't even know this girl. I gave her short, noncommunicative answers—telegraphing my grumpiness.

When I walked outside, it was almost as though I felt someone tap me on the shoulder, and I thought of my father. He would never have done that, I realized, no matter how bad a day he was having. Now, I make a point of going to that girl's line, listening to her recipes, answering her questions. I figure maybe she's lonely, and no one else listens to her, so I give her a few minutes of my time. Because that's what my father would do, because that's the kind thing to do.

What I have found, more and more, is that my father does tap me on the shoulder in small, everyday ways and in more profound ways. He is more of a constant presence in my life now, even though I'm on the other side of the country and he is thousands of miles away. But he's not really miles away. He's inside me, as our parents always are. For me, it's like coming to a fork in the road in terms of my perceptions of my parents. I could continue to wade through the troubled times, the things that didn't go right, or I could turn the other way and pick up the shiny moments, the ones that shimmer with a light I was blind to before. Those are the ones I want to put in my pocket, place under my pillow, keep dusted and safe on a shelf or an altar, and definitely in my heart.

I see now that for whatever ways my father might have stumbled in the monumental task of parenting, he provided a lantern in the darkness, a beacon, to show me the way home. And home is God. He sent us here, my father told me, and someday He'll take us back. I know that God will be ready to take my father home at some point, but because of what he taught me, because of the lessons in faith that I hold close, I'll know where he is. I'm certain I will see him again—on the other side, which he used to describe to me in green, magical stories.

I'm struck by how many times I listened to him tell me that people were created in God's image, that we are all God's children. Maybe at one time I chalked it up to biblical quotations, or the language of a churchgoing man. But when he frequently referred to John Hinckley as "misguided," I felt the weight of that word—the weight of what it said about my father. He never expressed anger or hatred toward the man who had shot him—he expressed pity. He knew in his soul that even Hinckley belonged to God. That knowledge leads to forgiveness; it transforms and heals.

Lives can then be constructed from Love, rather than from fear or vengeance. If one truly believes that everyone on this earth is a child of God, then however terrible an individual's deeds might be, the deeds themselves can be seen as tragic life choices, not as reflections of that person's soul.

The Vedas, the ancient Hindu scriptures, say, "Deep within each of us is a God in embryo. It has only one desire—it wants to be born." My father may never have read the

Vedas or heard those words, but that doesn't matter because he lives them. He looks at people by looking past their deeds to who they really are. Maybe not every moment of every day—he is, after all, human. But I've seen him do it again and again, enough to be impressed by it, enough to want to emulate it in my own life.

I've seen him do it to me. Following the book tour for my autobiography, I saw my parents again after a long estrangement. It makes sense to me that it happened that way. Despite what was extracted in the press, I had written about trying to move away from blame and judgment to the calmer waters of understanding. I'd written about looking at my parents differently, trying to see them in a new light, paying more attention to their backgrounds, to what shaped their lives. I had written about letting go—of childish assumptions that parents should be perfect, of adult judgments that parents should just stop being parents at a certain point. That was my motivation, that was the energy shaping each chapter. And that was the energy that allowed us to come together, even though we still had some wounds to heal.

I had been working so hard at trying to master all this—letting go of judgments, melting into the idea of forgiveness—stumbling along the way, I have to admit—that I didn't notice the seeds of my endeavors had been planted decades earlier, by my father.

I pictured a beautiful temple on a hill, filled with light from God that I hoped would spill into my life. I imagined myself climbing higher and higher. But I should have glanced back over my shoulder. Behind me was a tall, sheltering tree, planted from seed long ago. It was waiting for me to notice it, waiting for me to seek shade under its canopy. It was the way my father had chosen to live his life.

One thing I didn't want to do when I saw my parents again was enter into a conversation about what went wrong, or who was to blame in the past. We have since found avenues for that conversation, and others I never thought we'd be willing to have. Particularly my mother and I have been able to emerge from the tangled brier of our past together, into a clearing where Love was waiting for us to find it. But two years ago I felt that any airing of grievances would only keep us entrenched in old battlegrounds. If I had thought to look upward, to the branches of my father's life and character, I would have known that he never intended to wade onto old battlegrounds. He had his eyes set on stars, not on the dust of past wars.

I went to my parents' house for dinner, along with my brother, Ron, and his wife, Doria. We were sitting outside on the patio, and I looked over at my father. His eyes met mine, and what I saw there told me it only mattered that we were together. The past was somewhere behind us. It had no place right then, on that summer evening when a prayer of his was emblazoned on the horizon as gloriously as the sun that was setting at that moment. He wanted us to be together as a family, and we were.

There was no past, there was only that one glistening moment, and I thought, This is what it means to live in the present. I hooked onto him right then, like Wendy holding on to Peter Pan—I learned to fly over the past into the bright blue space that was right in front of me.

There was a story on the news recently

about the technology of virtual reality. Disabled people were taught, through virtual reality, how to navigate their wheelchairs, or even how to exercise their damaged arms by playing the violin—not a real violin, a virtual reality violin—an image crafted from air and imagination. But tell *them* it wasn't real, I dare you. That evening, my father transported me, with the look in his eyes, to a world I wanted to inhabit.

When I was young, my father would tell me that God never gives us more than we can handle. At the time it was a frightening thought to me. I would lie in bed at night and try to convince God I couldn't take very much, so He should really take it easy on me.

Obviously, God thought my father could take on one of the toughest challenges to his faith. To know that someone aimed a gun at you with the clear intention of taking your life, and to hold to the idea that buried inside that person is a pure soul—"a God in embryo"—is a challenge few could meet. I'm not sure I could. But my father did. Even while lying in the hospital with a surgery scar winding around his torso from the doctor's frantic efforts to save his life, he believed that, while John Hinckley had committed a hideous crime, he was still, at his core, a child of God.

My father was right when he called Hinckley misguided. Hinckley had forgotten, somewhere along the line, who he was and who had created him. Ronald Reagan knew more about the nature of John Hinckley's soul than Hinckley may ever know. That's why he could forgive him. It was less an act of generosity and more a result of seeing past the rubble, the darkness, the madness, to that one tiny ray of light burning deep within another human being.

During his recovery, my father said he believed he had been spared for a reason. He said, "The rest of my days belong to God." He said he knew he had more work to do here. I don't know what his specific ideas were; a safe assumption is that he was thinking along political lines. But I have my own ideas.

If someone can be brutally shot, survive, and articulate forgiveness in the simple and exquisite way my father did, I can think of no greater gift to the world. I know, when I recognized his ability to forgive, there was a deep shift of priorities inside me. My life continues to change as a result of that lesson. I feel my spirit reshape itself around my father's words.

Obviously, the world would be a different place if his attitude were more pervasive. So it starts with a seed, I suppose, which is probably how my father regards it. No big deal, he probably thinks, it's just what I believe. But seeds turn into trees and, if we're lucky, forests. That one statement, that one moment in time, changed at least one life. I walked out of my father's hospital room a different person, wondering if I could start a forest with that one precious seed I held in my hand.

Maybe everyone feels that, in some way, a John Hinckley has entered his or her life. The ultimate challenge in terms of forgiveness. This person may or may not have committed an actual crime, may or may not have wielded or aimed a weapon. There are emotional crimes and subtle, insidious weapons people use against each other. They are no less deadly, and they still bring you face to face with the same question: Can you find God in the person who became your enemy?

In November of 1993, I realized that I had met my John Hinckley. God had given me my biggest test yet in the lesson of forgiveness. At that point my father's words began echoing in my head. Not only had I met my John Hinckley but I was engaged to be married to him. His crime was getting me to trust him, to believe in him, while he was busy scheming behind my back. His weaponry was seduction and an astounding capacity—particularly for one so young—for dishonesty and subterfuge. My mistake was ignoring the red lights that were blinking furiously at me.

Looking back now, I remember one narrow moment when perfect clarity tried to get through. I realized that I would be embarrassed to introduce him to my father. Before I could absorb the full weight of that, before I could see how clear a warning sign that was, I chased it away.

At the eleventh hour, a week before we were going to be married, I found out about illegal financial dealings, violent tendencies, and various other seedy aspects of his past. It ended one horrible night when I had to get the police to force him to leave my house. I was more frightened than I had ever been. I sat in the yard, staring up at a quarter moon while a sympathetic police officer was inside the house, trying to get this man to leave, and I prayed. I prayed hard, that God would forgive me for my blindness and rescue me from the danger I had waded into so foolishly.

Sometime after midnight, when the man I had planned to marry was gone, I locked all the doors and windows (I'd had the locks changed that morning so he couldn't use his key), and I broke down crying. I asked God how I would ever be able to forgive this man. I knew I had to because it was the only way to sever myself from him forever. Hatred is a magnet, and I didn't want to pull him toward me—I wanted to be free from him. I didn't even want him brushing past my life again.

I knew, intellectually, what I had to do, but I didn't know how to do it. That's when my father's words came back to me, as if they were carried on the wind—across miles, across time, across all the angry, enraged emotions that were bubbling up inside me. I had to heal, and in order to do that, I had to forgive.

After all, I'd just been humiliated and used, not nearly assassinated.

I would be less than honest if I said that I have succeeded completely, reached the mountaintop, let it all go, extinguished all the angry embers in my heart. It remains one of my biggest challenges. On the spiritual ladder, my father is still many rungs ahead of me. There are moments when I can almost grasp it, when the smoke clears and I see that, somewhere in the depths of that man's soul, a tiny ray of light shines, and that light is of God. I try to be a student of those moments.

My father is with me every day, and nightly, whispering through my sleep. His lessons, and his words that remain a testament to his willingness to forgive, are my treasures. I tuck them inside my heart, hoping they'll grow and establish a domain there—put down a flag on the angry little moon my heart sometimes is and proclaim "one giant leap for mankind." I put them under my pillow at night and hope they'll seep into my dreams— maybe I'll wake up a little bit lighter. During the day I carry them in my pocket, where they can rattle around and remind me of who I can be if I keep my eyes on the mountaintop. And I keep my windows open, so that if I get careless and let them drift off, they'll be able to flutter back in and land someplace where I'm certain to find them.

3

❧

I have a friend who, for most of his adult life, was a Presbyterian minister. He recently stepped down from his ministry, but he remains active in church affairs. I have told him, frequently through the years, that I think he is too spiritual for the church. He is neither dogmatic nor restrictive in his thinking. He is not judgmental; rather, he is generous and curious.

I have a similar feeling about my father. I think his nature was too spiritual for politics, even though I know he was destined to step into that arena—born for it, I think. The world of politics doesn't focus on a person's light. Politics prefers darker instincts, hunts for them, finances them. At least that's my view, and probably my prejudice. I look at politics, and I think I hear siren songs, luring people into deep waters so they will drown.

I was introduced to the world of politics at a fairly young age. From the beginning, I couldn't accept my father's participation in the political arena. Beneath my distress was a jumble of feelings, many of them selfish, many of them having to do with my ideological differences with my father. What I focus on now, and what I think was more disturbing than I realized at the time, is the sense that he was wandering into some dark, angry land.

Perhaps in the distant past politics was more focused on bettering the world; perhaps it even aimed for the light, attempted to find the high road. Perhaps . . . but I look at what it's been in my lifetime, and that has not been my experience. Politics—to my eyes—wallows in the mud, hides under rocks, sneaks around corners. It's about lions fighting for control of the herd. My father sees himself spiritually as a lamb of God. The tragedy of politics today is that Oliver North actually fits in perfectly. He was drawn to its baser levels. I'm sure it felt like home to him.

Despite my ideological disagreements with my father, I have always respected the fact that he had a vision for America. I actually didn't quarrel with the vision—a shining city on the hill, a strong, prosperous nation. Although I've quarreled with the implementation of that vision, without some kind of vision for a country, or a relationship, there is little hope. The political machine that grinds along from campaign to campaign is not about vision. It's about winning the race, knocking out the opponent, and running off with the prize.

The difference between my father and his political peers was never more obvious than at the 1992 Republican Convention. In the midst of what was the most bigoted convention I'd ever witnessed, there was my father, giving a dignified, unprejudiced speech, intended to unify, not attack.

My mother has since told me that he saw the direction the convention was heading, and deliberately tried to pull it back from the racism and judgmentalism that were becoming dominant. The sad thing to me is that he may actually have believed he could. He was supposed to go on earlier in the evening, in prime time, but the other speeches went on so long that, by the time he took the stage, the convention was deep in swampland. I watched the entire event, and what I choose to focus on is that my father's speech had a dignity that didn't belong in that room.

Ironically, it was politics that forced my father to get beyond his fear of flying in planes, a fear that had been formidable. It's actually difficult for me to imagine his being afraid of anything, but he's said he was, so I won't argue. When I was younger, our family excursions were always by car or train. During the time he ran for governor, it was unavoidable; he had to put his fear aside and get on a plane.

He didn't make a big deal out of it; he seemed just to accept that it was a fear he had to get over. He seemed to glide past it; at least that's how it looked to me. Then he told me that every time the plane took off and landed, he closed his eyes and prayed.

"Do you pray that the plane won't crash?" I asked him, assuming that would be a logical thing for which to pray.

"No," he answered. "I pray that whatever God's will is, I'll be able to accept it with grace, and have faith in His wisdom. We're always in God's hands. Sometimes it's hard to accept that, so I pray that He'll help me just to trust in His will."

It was such a clear lesson in the language

of faith. I went into my room, stared out the window at a cloudy sky, and thought about what I had just learned.

What my father had communicated to me, through his words and between them, was that he believed God was in charge of his fate and the fate of everyone on the plane. He had told me once before that *when* we die is God's business. So it wasn't his place to second-guess God or to try to sell Him a particular agenda by praying, "Please don't let the plane crash."

And I thought of this, too: If I were falling through the sky, falling toward my death, would I want my last moments to be spent screaming at God for not obeying my wishes, or would I want to exit this earth in a moment of silent communion, a prayer for grace and acceptance? The latter definitely seemed like a better way to go.

My father has chosen, on a daily basis, to try to accept the will of God. He reminded me often that we do have free will. To him, that means a person can choose to trust in God's wisdom, accept it, and learn whatever lessons are being presented at any given moment, or that person can kick and scream and shake his fists at the heavens.

I don't know if I ever heard my father use the word *surrender,* but I find myself using it these days. And I realize more and more that there is nothing passive about surrendering to God. It's difficult, and the excuses not to surrender—to shove God out of the driver's seat and say, "Excuse me, I'll drive"—never seem to end.

I think of my father, sitting on an airplane, eyes closed, asking for the grace to surrender and trust. That's faith in its strongest form. And what feeds it is an understanding that a relationship with God is not supposed to mean that you hand Him a shopping list and expect to get every item on it.

My father used to say, "Ask and you shall receive," and "God answers all prayers." But, he quickly reminded me, there are no guarantees as to what we'll receive after we ask, or what the answer will be to the prayers we've spirited up to Heaven. In other words, we get answers, but not always ones we like. We're not meant to know everything, my father said, or to understand all God's reasons. We're just supposed to have faith that God knows His reasons. "Through a glass darkly . . ." I was always trying to get some more light on the subject. I was taught faith, and intellectually I understood, but, in one way or another, I was still arguing with it. I had a hard time accepting that the glass was dark because it was supposed to be, because God made it that way, because believing and trusting even when you can't see is what faith is all about.

I think we all get the lessons in life that we need. Whether we learn from them or not is up to us, but they are presented to us. The past year has tested me and challenged me to such a degree that I have found myself delving into my own history in new ways—going back to roots that I had either neglected or taken for granted. Learning about faith— really learning about it—was ultimately what came out of all the drama and unpleasantness, and it's not an accident that my father's voice whispered in the background. He probably wouldn't have made it so hard on himself, but then his faith has always been stronger than mine. I hope mine is stronger now as well.

There is a book by John Harricharan entitled *When You Can Walk on Water, Take the Boat.* The title sums up what the book is about, and I've been meaning to tell my father about it, simply because I think he'd smile and nod and know exactly what the author was saying, in the title alone.

Faith is the tonic that stops people like me from trying so hard. When I just give in to God, things work better. When I frantically try to prove myself, nothing goes smoothly. I think the reason my father has been called the Great Communicator is that, when he gets onstage or in front of a camera, his ability to express himself is effortless. It comes through him; he doesn't feel he has to prove himself. The power is there, the talent is there; he can afford to take the boat.

If my father and I were standing by a riverbank (carrying on with this analogy) and we were both able to walk across the water to the other side, I would want to march across that river—to prove I could, to ensure that the ability was still there, and because I would mentally create disastrous scenarios about boats. The boat might spring a leak, I would argue. Or the oar could fall overboard, or hit one of us in the head. My father would just climb into the boat, look back at me with a puzzled expression, and ask why I was worrying about things that hadn't happened yet. And why did I need to prove anything? So you can walk on water, he'd say, that doesn't mean you have to do it every day. You can relax once in a while.

My father would frequently give me a puzzled look when I was spinning out on what-if scenarios. I must have seemed to him like a car spinning out of control. He would always say, "Why are you worrying about things that haven't happened?" And he was sincerely baffled by my paranoia.

If I were to answer him now, I'd say, "Because my faith is not as strong as yours."

I feel that, in the past year, I've been taught invaluable lessons about fear and faith, and how it's possible to get the two confused. I've started to call the year my "Watershed Year" just because it has a more positive ring to it than "the year from hell" or "the year I almost jumped off the Brooklyn Bridge."

It started with my decision to leave Los Angeles. That decision actually was based on faith; everything inside me was screaming to get out. I felt as though part of my spirit was turning to ashes there and my life would be richer on the East Coast. I felt it so strongly that I knew God would help me realize what had been a dream of mine for quite a while. From that point on, things started to get messy, and confused. And sometimes what I interpreted as faith was actually stark terror. I wasn't taking boats, I was jumping on anything that looked like it could float.

I chose a town in Connecticut, went there a few times to look for a house, and wasn't able to find anything. I can look back now and see the points at which fear started to wind its tendrils around me, cut off my air supply—cut off my faith. But I didn't see it then. I had my timetable set as far as when I wanted to move, and my house in California was on the market. Finally, I rented a house in Connecticut, sight unseen—unless you count Polaroids, which I don't. I told myself that I could make any house livable and even special; I told myself that I was going on faith. The truth was, I was going on fear. I was afraid I'd go through all that's involved with moving across the country and not have a place to move into. Faith would have been: I know the right place will come along, because this is the right move for me to make at this point in my life. And God will provide for me.

I ended up in a house I hated. Not only was it unattractive but there was something strange about it, almost eerie. It didn't help that I also ended up with the man I described earlier, who had followed me across the country, professing his love. The man who became my fiancé, my biggest lesson in forgiveness . . . my very own John Hinckley.

Some strange twists of fate conspired to clean up the mess I'd made, and in the process teach me what faith is really all about, and how far off the mark I'd been.

First, one New York reporter made it her mission to uncover all the dirt she could on my fiancé; her articles were vicious, but in the end they saved me from a disastrous mistake. Then another reporter joined in the fray and printed where I was living. By the next morning strange cars were lurking outside my house, someone in a car followed me when I was out running and almost ran me down, and my neighbors said other people had stopped them to ask which house I was in. I'd never heard of a journalist printing someone's address, certainly not in these times, when memories of Rebecca Schaeffer are all too clear. Within one week I was ridding myself of a man who I had planned to marry but who had become frightening to me, and I was going to move again after having moved from California barely three months earlier.

I felt as though everything were crashing in on me. Frightened and confused, I didn't know how to sort things out. I remember saying, as I lay in bed, "God, you have to take this. It's too much for me. Please help me." And I heard a quiet echo deep inside me say, "I already am. You could have asked earlier, you know." At that point I had a physical sensation of being lighter—so light, in fact, that no matter how the waters underneath me were roiling and threatening to drown me, I knew I would just keep floating.

That's it, I thought—that's what faith feels like. Suddenly I understood why my father always seems to be floating above turmoil and trouble. He is made lighter by faith, by knowing without any doubt that God will handle things. It wasn't that all my ragged emotions were suddenly mended, but a part of me was sailing over them, looking down at the events and the emotions that were causing me such pain. That part of me knew God was with me, and He wouldn't let me drown.

My new home had every good feeling that the previous house lacked. I was leaving a toxic environment behind. I thanked God for it every day as I was packing things up yet again. As grateful as I was, though, there was still the stress of moving and the humiliation of a romantic disaster played out in the press. I was holding myself together, getting through it, but at times not very well. I felt alone and beaten down, as though I were hanging on to a very ragged thread.

I have read that, in the darkest times of life, miracles are given room to appear. I have finally experienced that, and I am fortunate in that I was taught to embrace the possibility of the miraculous.

When I was young, my mother gave me a typewritten copy of the poem "Footprints." It might be one of the only glimpses she allowed me to have of her spiritual beliefs. I remember taking it to my father and reading it to him.

He listened to it as if he had never heard it before, although I know he had. He was enjoying my discovery of it, my acceptance of its message.

The poem reads:

I dreamed I was walking along the beach
    with the Lord,
and across the sky flashed scenes from
    my life.
For each scene, I noticed two sets of foot-
    prints in the sand;
one belonged to me, the other to the
    Lord.
When the last scene of my life flashed
    before us
I looked back at the footprints in the
    sand.
I noticed that many times along the path
    of my life,
there was only one set of footprints.
I also noticed that it happened at the
    very lowest
and saddest times in my life.
I questioned the Lord about it.
"Lord, You said that once I decided to
    follow You,

You would walk with me all the way.
But I have noticed that during the most
     troublesome times,
there is only one set of footprints.
I don't understand why in times when I
     need You most,
You would leave."
The Lord replied, "My precious child, I
     would never leave you during your
     times of trial and suffering.
When you see only one set of footprints,
it was then that I carried you."

I should have read that poem during those days when I was feeling so beaten down; I should have read it every hour, but I hadn't thought of it. Then one morning, after I had packed up nearly everything else in the house, I went into my writing room to start packing up manuscripts and notes and things I wanted to keep organized and intact. As I got to the door, I noticed a piece of paper on the floor, just inside the doorway, where I couldn't possibly have missed it. I picked it up, and it was the poem "Footprints"—the copy my mother gave me so long ago.

It's on a small piece of paper. The single-spaced type has faded over time, and the edges of the paper are worn. For years I have kept it in a wooden box on top of my desk. There are only three things in that box—the poem, the keys to my desk, and my passport.

I stood in the doorway, wondering if I had opened the box for any reason, but I knew I hadn't. Even as I wondered, went through a questioning stage in my mind, I knew why it was there, right in front of me. I needed to have my faith restored; I needed to remember that, even though I felt alone, I wasn't. God was carrying me.

I spent only a few minutes puzzling over how the poem got out of the box and onto the floor, placed so conspicuously. I was taught to believe in miracles; I was taught to believe that God can do anything. He created the Universe; taking a piece of paper out of a box and putting it on the floor is nothing.

Part of the magic of that event was the way it opened up avenues of healing within me—avenues that had been there all along. I had forgotten, and needed to be reminded.

As far back as childhood, I had been given the tools for healing. I had been taught to trust that God is always there, ready to carry us. In the midst of all the troubles I was going through, I had lost my faith. I felt very much like that lone set of footprints in the sand. I needed to do exactly what I found myself doing when I found the copy of "Footprints" in the doorway—I needed to sit down, cry, and turn to God. I needed to have my confidence restored, to know again that He had never deserted me, and would not. It was I who hadn't remembered Him.

I met a woman recently who told me that after her husband died, she was so consumed with grief she couldn't do anything. She couldn't attend to the business of death—the paperwork and the documents. She said that papers appeared before her—the exact ones she needed—from out of a locked vault. I smiled and nodded, never doubting her story. I remembered bending down and picking up a poem that my mother had given me, that had in deep, quiet ways bonded my family, carried us past our disagreements, made us all pause and think of God. Something precious and vital had been called up out of the past, out of our history together, and been placed in front of me at the exact moment when I needed it the most.

I think I know what my father would do if something like that happened to him—some mysterious occurrence that couldn't be explained away rationally. He'd get a faraway look in his eyes—that look of blue distance that always made me wish for wings so I could fly across it—and he'd say, "God works in mysterious ways."

I always wanted to hear about those mysterious ways when I was a child. I went to my father for questions about God and angels and anything beyond this earthly realm. I was given answers that were magical, that strayed into the mystical, and I never tired of them.

When I first read about Joan of Arc, I asked my father about the spirits that were said to have visited Joan in her bedroom at night and talked to her. I asked if that could happen. He said, "Oh, I think so. God speaks to us in different ways. He chose to send angels to her." This affirmation prompted me to spend many sleepless nights, waiting for white, filmy apparitions to enter my bedroom and give me a noble mission for my life's work.

He told me about leprechauns that come out and dance when there is a ring around the moon. I suspect that's why I still check on the moon to see when there's a ring around it.

He told me that in Heaven I would meet everyone I'd known on earth.

"But, wait a minute," I said, alarmed at this possibility. "What if I don't want to see someone again? David Lewis teases me on the school bus and calls me names all the time. I never want to see him again."

My father paused, sat down so that he was on eye level with me, and said, "Well, here's the thing. In Heaven, people won't really act the same. Someone who is mean to you here won't be in Heaven."

"People get nicer when they die?" I asked.

He laughed and paused again, probably asking for guidance on how to answer a child's question about the friendliness level in Heaven. Finally, he said, "I guess you could say that. When we're up there living with God, we're all a lot nicer."

I asked questions about God's nature, too—about whether or not He got angry or vengeful. Sunday school lessons about God commanding Abraham to go kill his son, and then changing His mind, had confused me. I didn't want to think of God as a prankster. My father's answers were sweet, simple, and reassuring. He told me that God is about Love; He loves us no matter what we do. We can talk to God even when we're in a bad mood or feeling angry and bitter. He carefully sidestepped my questions about God and Abraham and why a loving God would test a man so cruelly. I suspect he was as baffled by that story as I was.

At the time I don't think I appreciated the simplicity of my father's answers. I wanted more. I was always wanting more. Simplicity is often deceptive; it's usually a difficult and complex process to carve out a simple way of looking at things.

When I was a child, I was expecting to hear a complicated, intricate answer, so I thought he was holding back, not telling me the deeper, more personal aspects of his spiritual life.

I was wrong. Faith is simple; it's as clear and uncomplicated as a stream. In fact, it's very much like a stream—flowing over rocks, straight home to God.

When my parents were in the White House, I asked my father once if he'd seen Lincoln's ghost. The stories are legendary. Butlers and many others who have worked at the White House have handed down stories about seeing Lincoln float through the rooms.

"No," my father answered—a bit sadly, I thought. "I haven't seen him yet. But I do believe he's here."

Lately I've learned—through a friend who is obsessed with Lincoln's history—that Abraham Lincoln was very spiritual, and that, just before his assassination, he had dreams in which he saw himself dead. It made me wonder if perhaps my father really did experience something, see something while he was in the White House. Maybe he thought it would have been irreverent to talk about it with anyone, as though such a visitation should be held sacred, kept confidential. I think my father might be someone Lincoln would choose to visit.

What seems remarkable to me about my father's faith is that it appears to be effortless. Maybe someday I'll get to that point, but I'm not there yet. I've gotten it right sometimes—

had my hand on the brass ring, felt the peace of just trusting in God without question—but at other moments my hand has slipped off. I've started to gather together in my mind all the times I have seen faith at work in my life, felt the pull of miracles. I have stacked up the experiences, enshrined them, so I can remember the lessons, the feelings . . . so I can construct my life around them.

A few months before I left Los Angeles, I was watching a television interview with a journalist who was very articulate and intelligent. He was the one being interviewed, which I'm sure is an odd reversal for any journalist. I was particularly impressed by how gracefully he handled it. The more I watched, the more impressed I was. I began thinking that it would be interesting to meet him.

Accomplishing this would require some effort, or some strategy. All I knew was that he lived in New York. I considered calling the television station and asking for a mailing address. Then I thought about contacting him through his agent, or through one of the journalists he worked with on a regular basis . . .

I was getting exhausted thinking about it.
I saw what I was doing and consciously
stepped off the mental merry-go-round that
was making me dizzy and mildly nauseated.
Deliberately, I said, "Listen, God, this guy's
attractive, and I was thinking I might like to
meet him. But I figure that if I'm supposed
to, you can handle it. The decision is yours."

And I didn't give it any more thought.

The next afternoon I took my dog for a
hike in the Santa Monica Mountains. After-
wards, I drove home and pulled up to a small
restaurant where I frequently went for takeout
coffee in the afternoons. As I walked in, I
heard a voice I recognized, and there at the
counter, getting ready to leave with his takeout food, was the journalist I'd seen on television the night before.

Here's what amazes me, and what I hold
on to as an example of getting it right: I never
once thought, This is fate. This means we're
supposed to get to know each other, maybe
date, marry, pledge our undying love, buy
matching burial plots. I knew, the minute I
saw him, that this meeting had nothing to do
with him. It was between me and God. It was

almost as if I heard a voice in my head saying, Just thought you'd like to know what can happen when you have a little faith, when you surrender things to Me.

I did introduce myself to the man, and we talked for about fifteen minutes. It was pleasant and bland, not as scintillating as I had imagined it might be. But it didn't matter, because that wasn't what the encounter was about. When I went back out to my car, I found myself glancing upward, toward the sky. I felt my father's face etched beneath my own. I'd seen him do that so many times— just a quick glance, checking in with God, or saying thank you. That's what I said in that instant, as my eyes grazed the sky— Thank you, God, for reminding me that it's all up to You ultimately, and life's easier when I remember that.

4

As I'm writing this, a storm is gathering strength outside. The clouds are dark gray, the wind is screaming, thunder is rumbling in the distance—moving closer, I think—and rain is pelting the windows. When I was a child growing up in California, the winters were stormier, there was more thunder and lightning, and sometimes it rained for days. I remember lying in bed at night wondering if it would ever stop, frightening myself with images of biblical floods. Building an ark seemed a likely scenario.

"Will the earth be covered by water?" I'd ask.

"What if it rains for months?"

"How big is an ark?"

And about the thunder, I would ask, "Is God angry?"

"No," my father answered, choosing the last question above all the others. "He's just rolling over."

"Rolling over?"

"Yes," he said. "God is very big. He makes noise when He rolls over."

The storms passed with no need for an ark, and apparently God was content to lie still for much of the year. But night was the time when my fears took shape—became monsters crouched in the corners, or hiding in the closet, or worse—breathing beside me. The fear that never left me was my fear of death. It was so enormous, I thought it should be rumbling in the heavens; it was so enormous, I couldn't talk about it. I never asked questions about that. I just kept it to myself, letting it crawl over me at night, alone in my bed, where I would shiver and cry like a hostage in some icy prison.

If there has been a lessening of my fear, it's happened in the last couple of years, watching my father slip into his eighties with humor and serenity.

He commented after he turned eighty that "the days dwindle down to a precious few." I don't remember what that line is from, but I noticed, when I heard it from him, that the word *precious* was what stuck in my mind. I didn't pick up any fear from him, or resentment at the passage of time; I perceived an awareness that life *is* precious—every day and every moment of it. Ideally, we should all hold to that awareness no matter what age we are, but sadly few of us do.

When I called my parents last holiday season to wish them Merry Christmas, I said to my father, "I hope you have a great day."

"Oh, I will," he answered. "I'm looking forward to it."

I heard so much feeling in those words, I thought about them all day and into the night. He was truly looking forward to that Christmas Day, embracing it as the joyous occasion it's supposed to be, except many of us can't quite seem to see it that way.

It was my first Christmas in Connecticut, and I spent the day and the evening alone. I wasn't sad about it; I wanted to be alone. I was still recovering from all that had happened in November. In a way, I felt like I was with my father the entire day, because the sound of his voice echoed in my head.

I walked my dog along the beach in the afternoon, watched seagulls soaring above icy rocks and choppy gray waves. I thought about how much, and how little, life seems to change—the first year I could drive, I raced out of my parents' house on Christmas Day and drove down to the beach, to be alone. I wondered if, when I'm in my eighties, I'll still be doing that. My father is twice as old as I am. That used to seem like a huge expanse of time; now it seems like a blip on the screen.

By evening there were snow flurries. I built a fire the way my father taught me, with the right layering of paper and kindling, the right placement of logs. I opened a bottle of Cabernet—a wine I knew he'd like. The first time he ever let me taste wine, I was too young to appreciate it and spit it out in his glass. He didn't say anything, but knowing his taste in wine, I'm sure I ruined a glass of some expensive vintage. I've learned, though, and find myself going through the same wine rituals I learned from him—letting it breathe, tasting a small sip and savoring it.

With snow falling outside, I sat in front of the fire and thought about my decision to move away from California, across the country to New England. One of my reasons was that I was hungry for seasons, and I think some of that hunger came from my father. Even though he loves California, speaks of it fondly and poetically, something about him has always made me think of seasons. Maybe it was his storytelling. Any good storyteller becomes the story, at least for a while.

My father could take a California Christmas—with glaring sun and sad, drooping palm trees—and turn it white and wintry just by spinning some tale of a Charles Dickens Christmas, with snow piled along the sides of the streets. He'd talk about trudging through the storm, pushing against strong winds, trying to see through the downfall of snow. I would feel my eyelashes start to freeze and my fingers start to go numb.

In my new house in Connecticut, there was a window seat in my bedroom. I would always open the curtains after I'd turned off the lights and sleep with the moon and stars spilling into the room. I did it because it made me feel closer to God, closer to the sky, and because, when the night is silver, it seems a shame to miss out on that beauty.

On Christmas night, there were no stars—

only a light fall of snow that collected on the windowsills and made no sound. I opened the curtains anyway, pulled the covers up to my chin, and thought about the night sky I couldn't see, the stars that were hidden behind the clouds.

My father taught me about the heavens, directed me to constellations. He traced the patterns of stars for me, showed me pictures in the sky that can easily be missed if no one takes the time to show you. He showed me Orion and Pegasus, the Big and Little Dippers. And the North Star—the dependable one—always there to guide me home should I be lost at sea. He used to say that to me—"If you're ever lost at sea"—as though I never would be. He said it with a smile in his voice and a wink in his eye. What he didn't know was I always felt I was lost at sea.

I used to dream of living in a lighthouse, and now many of the pictures on my walls are of lighthouses. They pull at me when I walk past them, steal my attention, make me dream and remember. I used to fantasize about my father coming to visit me in my lighthouse home, on some craggy shoreline with the sea raging below. I imagined that, if I lived there, I wouldn't feel lost at sea anymore. I would be stoic and alone, perched on my rocky cliff, blinking lights to other lost souls. See, I would boast to my father, now I guide in sailors who are stranded at sea.

Under the heading of "be careful what you wish for," I can look at my life and see the ways I've stayed on my rocky shore, luring in lost sailors with a promise of light. The truth is, I have never stopped feeling lost at sea.

I watched the snow fall outside my window on that Christmas night, and I realized that some of the dark waters I felt lost in had to do with my fear of death. Watching my father grow in serenity the deeper he gets into his eighties is becoming my beacon. Maybe I have finally found my lighthouse.

I wonder if he watches the sky differently now. The times I have been with him, it seems he does. There is more of a sense of wonderment, an amazement at the beauty that many of us are too busy to appreciate. So many of us go through our days, not taking the time to look up at all. My mother has said that my father frequently points out clouds to her, and shows her faces in them, designs that she can't see until he lets her into his imagination and draws the pictures for her.

When I was still living in California, there had been strong rains for more than a week. It was the end of January in 1993; streets had flooded, roofs had collapsed, and still the storms kept piling up over Los Angeles. On a Sunday morning, just as the chain of storms seemed to be ending, I went to my parents' house in Bel Air. I was talking with my mother, and the daylight coming through the windows kept changing from gray and dull to brilliantly sunny. My father was standing at the sliding glass doors, looking up at the sky. He made a comment about how the clouds were pulling apart, letting sunlight through, and then closing ranks again, plunging everything into shadow. There was awe in his voice—something rapturous and reverent.

I walked over to him and followed his gaze upward to the sky. It was magnificent; the clouds were gray but edged with gold, and it almost looked as if they were waltzing with the sun.

When I left my parents' house that day, I

made a promise to myself—to spend more time looking up, more time studying the clouds, the miracle of them, the way they can change the color and mood of the day. One of the storybooks I had as a child had a drawing of God blowing clouds across the sky. I remember showing it to my father. "Is this why there's wind?" I asked him. "God takes a deep breath and blows the air across the sky?"

"Yes," he answered. "It's how he cleans the sky."

My father has always looked at nature with an appreciative eye; I saw that frequently when I used to go horseback riding with him. He taught me how to spot the difference between a hawk and a buzzard, encouraged me to study their flight patterns. He showed me plants that, if dampened with water, produce suds and can actually be used as soap. "You see?" he told me, as we paused along a trail that he had cleared himself. "God thinks of everything."

I think he takes more time now, though, lingers a bit longer. My parents have a beautiful garden at their house, and I've heard my father speak rapturously about buds appearing in spring, flowers opening. It is wondrous, the cycle of nature that represents some of God's finest work. I used to wonder, when I was a child, how the plants knew it was spring; I thought God must whisper it to them.

I don't know why some people seem to lead charmed lives. Maybe it has something to do with listening to the whispers of their hearts, in the quiet moments that life affords us if we're calm enough to find them. Maybe they're the people who take a step back, leave a small space between themselves and the race of life—and fill that space with prayer. I've always thought my father had a charmed life, an angel's wings folded around his shoulders, a ray of light wrapped around his ankles, ready to pull him back from the edge. And I've tried to understand the source of it.

I used to watch him in church; when he said "Amen," it was like nothing I had heard before. He said it from some deep place within, with a gratitude that made me hear the word differently. He said it like a hymn. I was always uncomfortable in church—it wasn't my choice of where to go for communion with

God. But watching my father, eyes closed tight, saying "Amen" from the depths of his heart was like a church service in itself. These days, I think more and more about this charmed quality, this shiny X-factor that I want desperately to understand. I look for clues, aware that time is running out and, if I don't find them, I may always be left with unanswered questions.

Shortly before I moved from Los Angeles, I visited my father in his Century City office. He has a framed picture of his mother on the wall. I stood in front of the picture with him, compared his eyes with his mother's. I know she was very devout and taught him about the Bible. Her eyes look out from the photograph as if they were scanning the earth—level with the soil, straight ahead, following the white line on the highway. I glanced at my father, and he had that shimmery look again, as though he were following a vapor trail to some blue height that he alone knew about. His eyes were focused on his mother's picture, but something behind his eyes was focused elsewhere.

Maybe that's it, I thought, standing beside

him and just letting the silence be there—
maybe I have to train my vision and my attention. Then I thought about his age—he was
eighty-two at the time—and I looked at how
blue and clear his eyes were. And I noticed
how sweet his breath was. When a girlfriend
of mine had her baby, I noticed that the baby
had such sweet, soft breath, like a breeze
across a clean lake. I remarked to her that this
tiny being who had come out of her womb
just days before was so pure, it was as if life
hadn't tainted her yet, hadn't left any residue
there. Her breath came through her body like
a sweet wind, and her eyes were clear as water.
I thought of that as I stood beside my father.
Life wasn't leaving its residue on him anymore. In a way, it made me sad, because I
thought it meant he was leaving—withdraw-
ing from the earth and floating off to another
world—but doing it gradually because he's
gracious enough to know that's the kind way
to exit. But part of me wasn't sad. I saw great
beauty in it—a calm withdrawal, a graceful
exit that's played out in stages.

My mother has told me that one of the
things she has wished since her mother died

was that she had asked more questions, collected more answers. She said there are specific things—facts of her mother's life—that she'd like to know, and now can't. I look for more nebulous things from my father. I want to know what doorways he goes through when he looks at the sky and seems engaged in a deep exchange of thoughts. I want to know about the guardian angel standing behind him, hands on his shoulders, and how I can experience that in my own life. Of course, my father would just smile and shrug and tell me to look over my shoulder.

One of the principles in Buddhism is not to resist the ebb and flow of life, the belief being that only resistance brings suffering. I've always seen this quality in my father, but now I see it more. Life does bring us to its later stages, its older years, and it would seem that the way to go with that would be to become more reflective, more appreciative, to relax and melt into each moment. I see my father becoming less opinionated, less assertive about his opinions. Whereas before he would enter into a fervent political discussion at the dinner table, he now prefers to sit back, enjoy the company and the food.

I witnessed that the last Christmas I spent with them, before I moved east. Current topics like South Africa and Bosnia came up, and he had his opinions, but I was sitting next to him, and I watched his eyes; he really was more interested in the fact that the family was together for Christmas, and the food tasted good, and dessert was on its way.

I saw similar changes in my maternal grandfather toward the end of his life. Either his previously rigid opinions, his more dogmatic viewpoints fell by the wayside or else he just didn't feel the need to assert them. I think of it as putting on more comfortable clothes—looser, less restrictive—letting out the seams, and going without shoes.

That Christmas evening, as the entire family sat in the living room after dinner, the subject of Rodney King came up. I wasn't participating, because as a liberal I am definitely in the minority in a gathering of Reagans. Interestingly, my father was quiet as well. Then, at one point, he said, "Well, you know, I think people tend to forget that the man was drunk and driving ninety miles an hour through residential streets."

"That's true," I agreed, feeling that maybe it was safe to say something. "But that doesn't justify nine men standing around beating the hell out of him while he's on the ground."

My father paused, thought for a moment, and said, "No, I guess it doesn't."

It was a memorable moment for me, because I know at another time the discussion would have continued. But he was willing just to concede the point. It's easier that way. Winning arguments, scoring points in a discussion has to lose its appeal at some time. I think that's what has happened to him. He shrugged it off, moved on, because, after all, it was Christmas, he had his family around him, and life was good.

It seems as if I've been searching all my life for a magical elixir that would cure my fear of death. When my mother's father, Loyal Davis, was dying in 1982, there was a vigil of sorts for a few days. His kidneys had failed, it was just a matter of time; Ron, Doria, my mother, and I were at the hospital in Phoenix waiting for the inevitable moment. My father was unable to leave Washington right then. I thought that maybe if I were there at the moment of death, I might experience something that would erase my fear. I've known of people who saw light leaving a person's body and were profoundly altered by what they saw. They thought of death differently, with more acceptance, less fear. A friend whose parents are both gone watched his father die. He didn't see a light, but he told me that the moment itself was utterly peaceful. He said he witnessed on his father's face such serenity, such a calm surrender, that it was a moment of beauty, not horror.

"So are you afraid?" I asked him. "Having seen that, are you scared of death?"

"Not at all," he answered. "I have absolutely no fear."

I wanted that; I wanted to be transformed in that way. I thought it might happen in my grandfather's hospital room, but I fled before the moment of death. I lost my nerve and got on a plane back to Los Angeles. I whispered "I'm sorry" to my grandfather—just as the sun was coming up over the city where I had spent so many Easter vacations with him and my grandmother. I was sorry I was abandoning him, sorry I couldn't be more brave, sorry I was running away. I knew that he would die while I was in the air, which was exactly what happened.

I think sometimes of the ways in which my father has relaxed into life, with all its changes and problems; maybe that's the key to relaxing around the idea of death. I think of his confidence in God's love—God wouldn't make death a horrible experience, that's probably how he sees it.

My fear has remained, as black as ever, haunting me at night and crashing into my thoughts during the day. It has started to diminish a bit in recent years, though—there are moments when I can actually think, Okay, I know God will take care of me. Nothing as dramatic as seeing the light lift out of a dying person has transformed me. I have changed from observing my father at this stage of his life, when mortality is not just a concept but a companion.

I suppose, at some point, we all have to regard mortality as our companion, to make friends with it. We might as well, because the inevitable is not going to go away. Railing against death gets tedious, and living in fear is hardly productive.

At a party last year in California, a woman arrived dressed in white with a scarf tied around her head to conceal the baldness that was obviously from cancer treatments. The friend who had brought me there knew her and told me that she had already had a mastectomy and was now waiting to find out if she was a candidate for a bone marrow transplant, without which she would almost certainly die. This woman had such a light in her that, when I saw her walk in, I didn't see someone ravaged by cancer—I saw an angel.

I ran into her a few more times and had a chance to talk with her. She told me a story about when she was in the cancer ward at the hospital. After her mastectomy, as she was walking down the corridor, she passed a man whose face was disfigured by the cancer he'd had and the surgeries he had gone through. For a moment, she said, she saw past their bodies, past their diseases, past the sad environment of a cancer ward. She met his eyes, and met another soul.

I started to truly regard this woman as an angel, particularly because I seemed destined to run into her at moments when I was feeling blue or sorry for myself. Her courage, her lack of fear, and the beautiful light that emanated from her made me feel I was in the presence of an angelic being, and things snapped back into balance very quickly. She reminded me of what our spirits are really about.

After one of those times, I had a dream about my father. It must have been after she told me the story about the cancer ward, because I immediately connected the dream with her story.

In the dream I was walking along a beautiful, grassy hilltop. The light was soft and blue—evening light—and I saw my father up ahead, just standing there. I waved and walked over to him, but we didn't say anything. We just let our eyes meet. There was a calm, almost blissful feeling that we didn't need to talk because we were looking into each other's souls, and the acceptance, the connection that was there didn't need to be embellished. It was as though, in that dream, nothing happened, yet everything happened, just as it did when two people, stricken with cancer, met in a hospital corridor. In that instant, they met in a place beyond their physical bodies and their diseases. They met as two souls for whom death and disease weren't real because souls can't be sick or die. They met in a wide field, beyond the boundaries of the world, which is really where souls belong anyway.

I've asked my father several times about the hours after he was shot, when he was losing blood and they were racing to save him. I've asked if an angel came to him, or God, or if he saw a tunnel of light, traveled to some cloudy realm. He's always said no to my questions, although his eyes get a faraway look. I know I will never forget the light that emanated from him the next morning, the light that took away my fear the second I passed through the door of his hospital room. It was like coming out of a dark forest into a pool of sunlight. I go back to that doorway in my thoughts—often these days—trying to reexperience that light, hoping that some of it will spill over onto me, melt away the fears that still remain.

My feeling is that he went home and was sent back. For a brief time, he visited a realm of perfect, divine Love, and that visit is the light behind his eyes.

There is a beautiful passage in *A Course in Miracles* that reads:

> When you are still an instant, when the world recedes from you, when valueless ideas cease to have value in your restless mind, then will you hear His voice. So poignantly He calls to you that you will not resist Him longer. In that instant He will take you to His home, and you will stay with Him in perfect stillness, silent and at peace, beyond all words, untouched by fear and doubt, sublimely certain that you are at home.

Maybe when my father looks at the sky now, he goes home for a moment. I think he has a better idea of where that home is than I do. The fact that I still wrestle with my fear of death says to me that I'm still outside the gate. I got a glimpse of it in the dream I had—the calm that washed over me was so profound, I woke up thinking, This is what I should be feeling all the time. But I don't; it's still a wish.

Whether my father ever tells me about his experience in the hospital, I'll always believe he was transformed in some way. In his heart, and in the deepest places of his soul, I think he lives in a different place now.

The last time I saw the woman who, even in the throes of cancer, had such a light in her, I was getting into my car on Montana Avenue in Santa Monica. I had been missing her. I hadn't seen her in nearly a month, but I knew from friends that she was in the hospital having a bone marrow transplant. Then I saw her, walking into a store with her best friend, who had stayed with her through everything. I followed her into the store. When she turned at the sound of her name, I felt as though someone had punched me in the heart. It looked as if her light had dimmed. She was ashen, and had fallen back inside herself. I thought, What did they do to you? But I smiled and asked how she was.

"I'm wonderful," she said, and then I saw

that same light, a little fainter, but flickering around the edges. "I just got out of the hospital this morning," she told me. "And it's my birthday."

Her response reminded me of my father the morning after he was shot. When he saw the remnants of a sleepless, tearful night on my face as I entered his room, he said, "What's the matter? There's nothing to be sad about. I'm fine."

Perhaps both my father and this angelic woman traveled to the same place, were bathed by the same light, and returned to give the rest of us a glimpse of it.

When I was still living in California, I invited my parents to my house for dinner. Ron and Doria and a friend of mine were also there. I can't recall exactly how the subject of racial tensions and racially motivated violence came up, but I vividly remember my father discussing his feelings on the subject. He pointed out that America is a "melting pot" and that there really are no pure races left. We are all a mixture of various races and ethnic backgrounds, he said, so what better incentive do we need to strive for harmony? I thought of Rodney King during the Los Angeles riots saying, "Can't we all just get along?" My father went on at length about how we are all children of God, and God doesn't make distinctions between people on the basis of skin color. I said to my brother later, "I think he spoke at the wrong convention."

I couldn't help speculating what would have happened if Ronald Reagan had stood in front of the American public while he was president and spoken these same words. It is an appealing fantasy, but I had to pull myself back from it and recognize the beauty in his saying it now. I witnessed something very special; it happened in my home, at my dinner table, not on a stage in front of millions. But that doesn't lessen its importance.

I think some of my father's thoughts have been transformed as a result of having had time to reflect. He knows that his years are winding down. He sees that he is in the period of life when ideas and philosophies should be reexamined, looked at through a softer lens.

The process of aging can dredge up fear,

and frequently does. I have felt its pull in my own life—like a cold current as the years go by. One of my prayers is that I can age with the same sweetness, the same serenity, that I see in my father. He seems as calm as moonlight across the surface of a lake. I think of him whenever that icy, lake-bottom pull of fear starts dragging me down. I picture his eyes and I think of calmer waters, warmer currents, and soft, silvery winds. I believe with all my heart that those are my father's images when he looks back across the landscape of the life he has lived, and when he looks forward to the world that waits for him—a world more peaceful than this one.

5

Most of us, at some inevitable point, have to deal with the grief of our parents' passing. If we're lucky, we have years to ponder it, adjust to the concept, take care of whatever is unfinished. I have been thinking about grief lately—not in a terrible way, really—but I will confront it eventually. I observe my thoughts, sift through them, pay close attention to the experiences of others, and try to learn from those who handle grieving gracefully.

Years ago, when the actor Patrick Duffy lost his parents in a brutal murder, he said that, even though he would miss them terribly and was angry at the way they had died, death itself was not sad to him. He said he didn't regard death as something frightening or awful because of his faith and his practice of Buddhism. I was so moved by his ability to find some solace even in grief, and to let his spiritual beliefs anchor and balance him. I was reminded that my father had revealed a similar attitude almost thirty years ago.

I had gone out to the ranch with him on a Saturday, when I was about eleven or twelve. My mother and Ron didn't go on this particular day; it was just the two of us. We were planning to ride horses.

I remember the day was warm and sunny, and we rolled down all the windows in the station wagon. Over the roar of the wind through the car, my father was lamenting that he couldn't ride his horse and would have to ride another. His horse was in foal and was supposed to give birth any day. This wasn't a planned pregnancy. When my father's horse had come into season, our Appaloosa stud, who we thought was secure in his pasture, had broken through two fences to get to her, succeeding admirably.

There are some animals with whom you have a special bond. I've loved every dog I've ever had, but one or two have stolen my heart. It was that way with my father and this horse. She was a beautiful thoroughbred whom he had named after my mother—Nancy D. They had been through so much together. She was one of those amazing animals who seem to know more than they should. I have a photograph of my father jumping her over one of the jumps he built himself out at the ranch. Every time I look at that picture, I can almost hear him talking to her as she clears the jump.

When we arrived at the ranch, Ray, the ranch hand who had worked with my father for years, met us at the car. It was clear something was wrong. He'd been crying and started again.

Nancy D. had died suddenly during the night. We later found out that a virus had struck without warning. The illness had taken her and the Appaloosa foal she was carrying.

I can remember so clearly the sun on my back and the tears running down my face. I had grown up with this horse, she was part of the family, and I loved her. But when I looked up at my father, he wasn't crying; he was looking off in the distance with a sweet, sad expression on his face.

"Why aren't you crying?" I asked him.

"Because," he said, "I'm thinking of all the good times we had together, all the wonderful memories I'll have of her. Even though she's gone, I'll always have those."

I'm sure that, in the days that followed, there were tears. Maybe he cried in private, or with my mother—I don't know. But on that particular day, he showed me that grief has more than one color to it. There can be a sweetness to it, a cherishing of the memories death can't take away. I imagined, at the time, my father walking past his sadness to a river, where all his memories were tiny white sails, always afloat and always graceful. I imagine myself doing that in the future, and hope I'll be able to.

I choose to keep afloat the memories of horseback riding with my father and learning about animals and the land. Or bodysurfing with him in the ocean, taking the big waves because he did and I wanted him to be proud of me. Or listening to him talk about God as if He were a friend next door. Or the way his eyes looked beyond years of dissension and told me it only mattered that I was there. I choose to remember the times when there was only love between us, when nothing intruded upon that. I choose to keep the stars my father showed me polished and bright, and thank him every time I look up at the heavens.

Those moments are the priceless jewels of a lifetime. In the end, they are the only ones that matter.

When Richard Nixon died recently, I watched the funeral service on television. I was so overcome, my eyes were swollen for days. I puzzled over my reaction—I'd met Nixon, but I didn't know him. While the service itself was moving, my emotions seemed a bit excessive to me.

Then it dawned on me that maybe I was going through some of the messier stages of grief in advance—projecting, in a way, since the connection to my own life was unavoidable. It was a presidential funeral, with gun salutes, flags, and protocol . . . and my parents were sitting in the row reserved for former presidents and first ladies. Whenever the camera panned that row, I would study my father's face. I wondered what he was thinking, and I noticed how intently he was listening to the eulogies. Perhaps what I'm doing, I thought, is trying to clear the way for the lesson he taught me that day at the ranch—that sadness can be tinged with gratitude, for the times

that will live in memory, the moments that
remain treasures even after death.

My first experience with losing a friend to
death was when I was in college. My friend
died in a climbing accident after being
trapped on the side of the mountain in freez-
ing temperatures while rescue teams tried in
vain to get to him. Finally, he fell to his
death. He was twenty years old.

I was angry at God for taking him like
that, and shocked and upset at the suddenness
of having him there one day, and then learning he was gone. I called my father and somehow managed to explain what had happened.
I think I told him that, right then, I hated
God—how could He have let this happen?

"You don't know God's reasons," my
father said. "You're not supposed to know.
But your friend is with God now—eventually,
you'll know that."

Eventually, I did know it, and he was one
of the people I thought about when I listened
to Billy Graham's eulogy at Nixon's funeral.
Graham talked about seeing people on the
other side, about death not being final, and

people not being lost to one another. As the camera panned the small audience of people attending the funeral, I paid close attention to my father's face. The echo of his words was so close. He had told me, also, about feeling his mother's presence at times—softly, just a quiet hand on his back.

He's probably always known this, I thought. And he believes it with every fiber of his heart. I still have some reservations in my heart. Usually they only make themselves known in the dark hours of night—little, annoying thoughts that jump up and say, "Excuse me—how do we really know?" I'm working on them, though. I talk to them the way my father used to talk to me. I tell them they're not supposed to know, they're just supposed to believe.

And I return to some of my father's stories about the afterlife and the beautiful, lush landscapes I would find there. The animals would talk to me, he said—not like the rabbits at the ranch, who scampered away and wouldn't let me near no matter how sweetly I called to them.

Sometimes, when I was young, I would

find pictures of enchanted forests and angels swinging from golden ropes between the branches of trees.

"Will Heaven look like this?" I'd ask my father.

"Yes," he'd answer. "And right over there, beyond that hill, where you can't see it, is a lake, with swans . . ."

"And what's over here?" I'd ask, pointing to nothing on the page, but willing to see whatever he described to me.

"Over there is a castle, with jewels around the windows."

"Do dogs get to sleep inside the castle?" This was important information, because our dogs weren't allowed to sleep in the house, except during thunderstorms, and I thought it was terribly unfair.

"Yes." He nodded. "They have their own room."

I still think of these stories. They help me to sleep at night, they quiet my fears, and they remind me of who my father is.

6

In February of 1994, I was back in Los Angeles as part of the book tour for my novel *Bondage*. I was nervous about returning because I was going back as a visitor to a place that had been my home all my life. I didn't know what kind of emotions I would have. Would I feel any pangs of regret or nostalgia? Even if I didn't, it would be odd staying in a hotel in a city where I'd always had a home. I arrived on a Friday evening and had an interview scheduled for that night. In fact, my whole schedule was tightly booked, which gave me a slight sense of relief—maybe I wouldn't have too much time to ruminate.

It was two days before my father's birthday. I had a birthday card in my suitcase for him, although I hadn't called and made any plans to see my parents. I thought I might see them, but then I thought maybe I wouldn't, and I'd just mail the card and call on his birthday. I was not in a good frame of mind for making decisions of any kind. I was sleep-deprived, stressed-out from the book tour, and I had been dreading this return to Los Angeles for weeks.

When I got to the hotel, there was a message waiting from the journalist I was supposed to meet that night. He'd had an emergency of some kind and had been called out of town. I felt uneasy about the evening that lay ahead. If Los Angeles were still my home, I wouldn't have cared. But I was in a hotel, and memories were creeping in on me. I called a couple of friends, but since it was Friday night, they weren't home. I considered going to a movie, but that didn't really appeal to me. Okay, I thought, taking a deep breath and hanging up a few clothes, I'm not going to get upset about this. Whatever this evening is supposed to be will be made clear to me. I knew I had to calm myself down and have a little faith, because I was approaching a mild state of panic. I'd flown in from Chicago, and I couldn't remember when I'd last eaten, a common affliction on book tours. Of course, I was also so worn down I couldn't figure out if I was hungry, but eating something seemed a good first step.

I went to a restaurant in Venice, where I knew there were tables in the bar area so I could sit, unnoticed, in a dark corner. I ordered a salad and a glass of wine, watched the cars pass outside the window, and tried not to think in terms of making frantic plans just to ease my anxiety. As I was sitting there, I thought of one of the interviews I'd done in which I'd been asked the inevitable question about how my relationship is with my parents these days. In the course of answering, I said that I was most grateful to my father for teaching me to talk to God when I was a child.

But I've never told him that, I thought. I've never thanked him.

Suddenly I knew what I had to do that evening—I had to see my father and tell him, thank him, give him his birthday card. I went back to the hotel to call, not knowing if he were home or out of town. He and my mother had just been in Washington—maybe they were still back east.

I called, and my father answered the phone, which he only does if he's there alone. Otherwise, he lets my mother answer. I told him that

I'd just gotten into town and I wanted to see him for a few minutes, wish him happy birthday—could I come up right then? He said yes, and mentioned that my mother was in New York. It wouldn't have altered my plans if my mother had been there, but I think that there was a reason she wasn't. I think we were supposed to have that time alone.

The card I had gotten for him said, appropriately, "Faith is the light through the darkness." It was blank inside, and I had written, "Thank you for the gift of faith that you have given me."

When I thanked him for having taught me to talk to God, when I saw how moved he was at hearing this, I thought I was going to cry. Don't, I told myself. You can cry later—stay clear right now, because what's going on here is really important.

I asked my father if he remembered my mother giving me the poem "Footprints" when I was a child. "Yes," he said, getting that faraway look in his eyes.

I told him about finding it on the floor, out of its box when I hadn't opened the box, and how it had appeared just at the right time, when its message was what I needed so desperately. He didn't say anything for a few long moments, and as I was watching him I realized something: He's shy. My father is shy—it was such an astounding realization to me, because for most of my life I had misinterpreted that shyness as emotional distance, casualness about my emotions. I had let what I perceived as distance wound me when it wasn't distance at all. He was just being shy.

He became even more shy as he noticed me watching him. "I don't know what to say," he told me, apparently thinking I was waiting for him to say something.

"Oh no, that's okay," I assured him, snapping myself out of my own thoughts, where I had gotten lost. "You don't need to say anything."

"I had a talk with God just today," he said, "when I was flying back from Washington."

I wanted to ask what he'd talked to God about, but I think that's a rather invasive question. "Do you remember telling me how, when a plane takes off, you pray that whatever God's will is, you'll be able to accept it gracefully?" I asked him instead.

He nodded.

"That taught me so much about spirituality. Rather than praying the plane won't crash, just to pray for a state of grace no matter what happens."

He looked at me, and his eyes were twinkling a little. "Well," he said, somewhat sheepishly, "sometimes these days I pray it won't crash along with my other prayers."

"I think that's okay," I told him.

We talked for a few more minutes about prayer and having a relationship with God, but it was getting late, so I offered to say good night. When he walked me to the door, my father said, "God is always listening and watching. I know He's listening to us right now. He's looking down at us, and He's smiling."

Once, when I was young, I was out in the backyard at our Pacific Palisades home. I was on the swing set, trying to see how high I could go. It was a gray, cloudy day, and suddenly a small break in the clouds allowed a shaft of sunlight through, like a beam aiming straight for the earth. I looked up and thought a window into Heaven had opened in the sky; I thought God had parted the clouds to peer down and see how His children were doing.

The clouds parted a little on that February night, just two days before my father was to turn eighty-three. It was a window into Heaven—just a small space in which a beautiful exchange took place.

I cried all the way back to the hotel, more out of gratitude than anything else. I thought about the way events had arranged themselves—the cancellation of my interview, my father's happening to be at home. And I felt God's hand in my life as powerfully as I ever had. I had been given a small space in time in which to return a gift. Years ago my father gave me a gift of faith; he set something in motion in my life that has kept me tied to him, whether I knew it all the time or not. By thanking him, I returned the gift, and I also answered a question I should have answered a long time ago. I should have listened to my dream, called him up and told him I talk to God all the time. I should have run to his front door to tell him or written it in the sky. But I was given another chance.

*   *   *

I believe we choose our parents—on the other side, when we are functioning as the wise souls God intended us to be. We choose them to learn what we need to learn, which can bring both solace and sorrow into our lives on earth. I think I chose well, although I didn't always hold that view. I've learned from the disagreements and the conflicts that characterized my life with my family, and ultimately I vowed to ferret out whatever lessons were buried in the rubble. Most important, I learned as a child to turn my face to God, to look through the clouds, certain that I was looking through a window into Heaven.

The older I get, the more certain I am that there are windows into Heaven. Maybe that's what my father sees when he studies the sky these days. I'm sure his vision, when he looks up, is clearer than mine.

Still, when I see an opening in the clouds that looks like a porthole into another world— a golden, light-filled world—I stop whatever I'm doing and stare at it. I move around, trying to find just the right angle, sure that if I do I'll catch a glimpse of God.

*   *   *

When I used to go horseback riding with my father at our ranch in Agoura, there was one hill we would always gallop up. We'd start in the field below and give the horses their heads so they could go as fast as they wanted. At the top of the hill, we could look down on the neighboring ranch—a beautiful valley with a lake.

As we galloped up the hill, my father was always ahead of me. I remember watching his back, with the sound of horses' hooves thundering in my ears. I think of that image now as a metaphor for what I've learned, and continue to learn, from him about forgiveness, faith, moving beyond fear, and moving through grief. I imagine myself following him up a hill.

And I think, also, of sitting at the top of that hill with a peaceful, green valley below. It felt as if we were, for those few minutes, in another country.

There is a quotation from the Sufi poet Rumi: "Out beyond ideas of right-doing and wrong-doing, there is a field. I'll meet you there."

A few times during my life with my father, I've met him in that field. The night I sat with him and thanked him for teaching me to talk to God was one of those times. Meeting him in my dream, on a hilltop, was another. There have been others—too few, part of me thinks, but they glow in the dark, so why count? Moments like that stitch together a relationship; they are the strongest threads, the ones that last through years and quite possibly through lifetimes.

When I think of my father, I think of him in that field. I've chosen to think of him there, despite the echoes outside its boundaries. Learning lessons in this life can be a messy, noisy process. But there will always be that one green place, that one meadow where no words are needed, where there is just wind, warm light, and a feeling of having arrived home.

Epilogue

It seems appropriate that, just when I think this book is finished, it isn't.

A week ago I had to make the painful decision to put my dog to sleep. I had known for months it was coming, but that didn't make it any easier. Age, health problems, and a deteriorating hip combined to create a look in her eyes that was unmistakable. Help me, it said. I don't want to be here anymore.

She was my best friend for ten years. Mine was the last voice she heard as she slipped away; I felt the life go out of her as I held her. And I knew, as I felt a chasm open up inside me, that in her death, as in her life, she was carving out a place in my heart that would always belong to her. She taught me about death, offered me the experience I had run away from before.

It was raining when I walked out of the vet's office with a friend who had been generous enough to go with me. The sun had been out when we walked in—with Sadie, walking beside me the way she had for a decade of my life. Three of us walked in, chased by sunlight; only two walked out, into a relentless rainstorm.

I thought of her running across hillsides and meadows in the rain, the way she used to before the pain in her hips slowed her down. I knew, wherever she was, she was running again, free from pain, free from the fear that had started to hold her hostage. And I thought of my father, looking up at the sky when he was told his horse had died.

I do that now—often—whenever some deep, silent scream asks where Sadie is. I notice that my eyes turn upward to the sky—to a white cloud floating past or to empty, endless blue.

I know where she is. I learned it from my father that day at the ranch when his eyes turned distant and then glanced up. I thought of calling him, crying to him that this hurts so badly. But I haven't called, because he already gave me the tools to get through this, to understand it. Asking again would only be asking for a refresher course, and it occurred to me that at some point the teacher has to walk away and let the student stand alone.

I haven't called for another reason—because my father's going through the changes that life brings to us in its late stages. I'm not even sure what some of those are, but I know they must be huge. I have a feeling of reverence about my father being in his eighties—a feeling that I want to whisper, take soft steps, not intrude too much. He's like a stately old cathedral to me now; I sit in a back pew, in the shadows, bow my head, and pray for all of us . . . but not loudly enough to ruffle the air.

So I'm learning about grief, and watching myself go through its stages, peel away its layers. Each day is a little different. It was slightly astonishing to me to realize that, while I have experienced sadness in my life, I have never gone through grief before this. It's the ultimate growing-up experience. Much of this has marked a passage for me, a belated one probably.

I grew up with animals. We always had dogs, and there were times when I was witness to the painful decision my parents had to make about putting a dog to sleep when the quality of his or her life had gone downhill. But the burden of the decision was theirs, as was the pain of carrying it out—that awful last drive to the vet's office. I don't even know if they remained with the animal—I never asked.

This time it was my turn, and I had to accept the responsibility—alone. Even more dramatically, I had to stand in front of my own fear of death and stare it down. I had walked out of my grandfather's hospital room, just hours before he died, too frightened to stay. But I couldn't abandon my dog and let her make that passage alone. We were too bonded; too much of our ten years together had gone by with just the two of us.

She went like a soft wind. It was so peaceful. Suddenly, her rib cage was still—she was still. I whispered to the vet, "Is she gone?" Whispered because it would have seemed irreverent to speak up. The vet listened for her heartbeat and nodded. I closed my eyes for the briefest of moments and listened to her soul leaving, flying off to God, who I knew would love her as much as I did, although the motherly addendum to my prayer was "Please take special care of her. She doesn't like to be alone, and she hates loud noises." I would guess that Heaven's probably a pretty quiet place, but I just wanted to make sure.

And then I waited for the deluge—the onslaught of emotions that I knew would take me on some kind of journey, and would ultimately change my life forever.

It came first with the rain—with the sky letting loose tears to match my own. My sadness felt as big as the sky. It came with an ache so deep I thought I would bleed to death. It came with the flood of memories, and the guilt—normal, they tell you, but that doesn't lessen it. I had decided to end a life; I had carried out the decision. She'd asked me to help her; she had spoken to me with her eyes, and with all the things she couldn't do anymore. I couldn't wait until she was completely crippled, a realization that was a straight shot back to my childhood—my father taught me that animals have dignity and they shouldn't be allowed to lose that. But the power of that responsibility, the enormity of that decision, was terrifying.

I'm discovering for myself now the sweeter side of grief. The glimpse I got from watching my father so many years ago is taking shape in my own life, rearranging it a little each day. It feels like small steps sometimes, but I can feel it happening. The brighter memories eventually bubble to the surface and stay there, and my sadness has taken on a quiet calm. I remembered the other day that the drive home with my father after he learned about his horse's death was quiet and dreamy. I remember leaving him alone with his thoughts, as if he had hung a Do Not Disturb sign around his neck.

I find myself taking a step back, and studying all the different colors of this grieving process, because I know it's terrain I will visit again. My dreams at night have become tangled and confused—Sadie and my father end up in the same dream, with circumstances and time sequences jumbled and out of place.

I begin each day by asking God to help me through the day, because there is a numbness I can't fight—a slow tide that I just have to ride; I can't go any faster. I am doing what I was taught to do—I'm letting God carry me.

And it's opened the way for miracles—small ones, maybe, but important to me. A couple of people I had been unable to forgive—people who had been unfair and cruel to me in a business context—were put right in front of me. One of them doesn't even live on the East Coast. He lives in California, but there he was, walking toward me on Madison Avenue at a point in my life when I didn't have the energy to be angry or to hold a grudge. I watched myself be friendly and cordial, I watched myself float over the past, and when I walked away I knew that God was smiling.

There are no accidents, my father always told me. I was given a chance to heal past grudges because I was open to it, because I was starting each day by surrendering it to God.

I keep looking at my fear of death, checking on it—is it still there? Was it just an illusion, or has it really gotten smaller? I check it like an old wound—does it still hurt? I return to the moment when Sadie's soul floated out of her body, floated out of my arms. I return to the hush that fell over everything. The other night, just before I drifted off to sleep, I had a sweet, serene confidence that being with Sadie at the moment she passed on has made me less afraid of death, and that if I found out tomorrow I was going to die, I would think of her, waiting on the other side of the door for me—the way she used to before it was too painful for her to get up.

I reinforce myself often with that image, and I embellish it, imagining who else might be waiting for me on the other side of the door. I remember my father talking about death as passing through a doorway, and I would guess his thoughts traveled along the same paths as mine.

As much as I have gained from my father's stories and comments about God and the angels, I've also learned from his silences. Silence is like the blank space in a painting, or a pause in a piece of music—it's important. On the long, quiet drive when he and I carried home the sad news about his horse, I couldn't know exactly to what island his thoughts had sailed, what retreat he'd found. It was something I had to experience on my own.

I know now, because hours drift by sometimes and my thoughts are in another world—
of memories, and sadness, and the ache that I
know will lessen with time. I'm a little more
detached these days, a little calmer. I watch
the world from a slight distance, and with a
keener eye. Something changes inside when a
life expires in your arms—things that used to
seem weighty and important aren't anymore.

Ancestry is powerful medicine. There was
a time when I tried to ignore it, but it was
always scratching at my window. Now I keep
my window open in all seasons. Floating in
the mist behind me are generations of sturdy
Irish, who sustained themselves with storytelling and a faith in magic. One of them
handed some of this down to me, and it's been
powerful medicine.

I had the sense, while writing this book,
that there was a presence standing behind me,
with hands on my shoulders. I thought about
my father's story—waking up in England
with a feeling that someone was behind him,
keeping him safe. And I say a silent prayer of
thanks, for the legacy that he has given me—
the legacy of faith. I look over my shoulder

more often now, I feel hands guiding me, keeping me safe, and I gain strength from the stories he told me. He took out a box of paints and painted a picture of Heaven that captured a child's imagination. In adulthood, I'm trying to let it color my life.

RONALD REAGAN

Nov. 5, 1994

My Fellow Americans,

I have recently been told that I am one
of the millions of Americans who will be
afflicted with Alzheimer's Disease.

Upon learning this news, Nancy & I had to decide
whether as private citizens we would keep this
a private matter or whether we would make this
news known in a public way.

In the past Nancy suffered from breast cancer
and I had my cancer surgeries. We found
through our open disclosures we were able to
raise public awareness. We were happy that as
a result many more people underwent testing.
They were treated in early stages and able to
return to normal, healthy lives.

So now, we feel it is important to share
it with you. In opening our hearts, we hope
this might promote greater awareness of this
condition. Perhaps it will encourage a clearer
understanding of the individuals and families
who are affected by it.

At the moment I feel just fine. I intend to live
the remainder of the years God gives me on this
earth doing the things I have always done. I will
continue to share life's journey with my beloved
Nancy and my family. I plan to enjoy the
great outdoors and stay in touch with my
friends and supporters.

Unfortunately, as Alzheimer's Disease progresses, the family often bears a heavy burden. I only wish there was some way I could spare Nancy from this painful experience. When the time comes I am confident that with your help she will face it with faith and courage.

In closing let me thank you, the American people for giving me the great honor of allowing me to serve as your President. When the Lord calls me home, whenever that may be, I will leave with the greatest love for this country of ours and eternal optimism for its future.

I now begin the journey that will lead me into the sunset of my life. I know that for America there will always be a a bright dawn ahead.

Thank you my friends. May God always bless you.

Sincerely,
Ronald Reagan